The Complete Proverbs 31 Woman

Susan J Nelson

ISBN:
ISBN-13: 978-1720422426

DEDICATION

To the love of my life, my biggest supporter, my rock and my built-in comedy show, Mike. I love you more than all of the stars in the sky and praise God every day for giving me the beautiful gift of you.

To Jesus, my Lord and Savior. I am nothing without you.

CONTENTS

ACKNOWLEDGMENTS

This book would not have been possible without the unending and loving support of my husband, Mike.

Thank you to the readers and fans of Woman of Noble Character who remind me daily why I do what I do.

The Complete Proverbs 31 Woman

Verse-by-Verse Discussion on What it Means to be a Woman of Noble Character in Today's World

Proverbs 31:10-31

A wife of noble character who can find?

    She is worth far more than rubies.

Her husband has full confidence in her

    and lacks nothing of value.

She brings him good, not harm,

    all the days of her life.

She selects wool and flax

    and works with eager hands.

She is like the merchant ships,

    bringing her food from afar.

She gets up while it is still night;

    she provides food for her family

    and portions for her female servants.

She considers a field and buys it;

    out of her earnings she plants a vineyard.

She sets about her work vigorously;

    her arms are strong for her tasks.

She sees that her trading is profitable,

and her lamp does not go out at night.

In her hand she holds the distaff

and grasps the spindle with her fingers.

She opens her arms to the poor

and extends her hands to the needy.

When it snows, she has no fear for her household;

for all of them are clothed in scarlet.

She makes coverings for her bed;

she is clothed in fine linen and purple.

Her husband is respected at the city gate,

where he takes his seat among the elders of the land.

She makes linen garments and sells them,

and supplies the merchants with sashes.

She is clothed with strength and dignity;

she can laugh at the days to come.

She speaks with wisdom,

and faithful instruction is on her tongue.

She watches over the affairs of her household

and does not eat the bread of idleness.

Her children arise and call her blessed;

her husband also, and he praises her:

"Many women do noble things,

but you surpass them all."

Charm is deceptive, and beauty is fleeting;

but a woman who fears the Lord is to be praised.

Honor her for all that her hands have done,

and let her works bring her praise at the city gate.

Introduction

In our modern society, many scoff at the idea of the Proverbs 31 woman. They say that it does not relate to women today. As you will see in the following chapters, I wholeheartedly disagree.

The Proverbs 31 wife is alive, well, and living in your city or town.

She is the one that has a three-cord strand marriage with God at the center.

She is the one that views her husband and family as her first ministry.

She is the one who places our promise of heaven above earthly things.

As we go, verse by verse through Proverbs 31:10-31, it is my desire that you find the Proverbs 31 woman within you.

I pray that you learn practical ways to fear the Lord and be the wife that God desires for you to be.

A wife of noble character, who can find?

She is worth far more than rubies.

Proverbs 31:10

A Wife of Noble Character

Wow! This biblical ideal wife can do everything, it seems! She gardens, cooks, sews clothing for her family and drapes for her home. She helps the needy and is an entrepreneur and she does it all while looking amazing. It is easy to read this scripture and feel overwhelmed or defeated. I mean, HOW in the world can you do all of that with pets, work, kids and their activities and a needy husband? You may dismiss it altogether thinking that being a Proverbs 31 woman just is not feasible in today's society.

Well, dear friend, I am here to tell you that you CAN live a Proverbs 31 life and it is what God wants from us as his daughters. Granted, we do not have to plant our own fields (hey, we have grocery stores now) or sew your own clothes (hello, Macy's!), but you can live a godly life pleasing to Him, in the image of the Proverbs 31 woman, in 2018. Now, there is nothing wrong with planting a garden or sewing your own clothes. I have a huge garden that we enjoy the fruits of every year, but that is not what this is all about.

Becoming a Proverbs 31 Woman

So what IS it all about? Being a Proverbs 31 godly woman is about living a life that is one of ministry. It is putting God first and your husband second and everything - yes, even your children - after that. It is about being industrious instead of idle. It is serving your husband, your family and your community. It is not about having a spotless home or wearing the latest fashions. Again, there is nothing wrong with those things, but it is a matter of putting your priorities in order.

The Bible uses the root word for "virtuous" or 'excellent" four times to describe women. In one of my favorite books of the Bible, Ruth, Boaz says to Ruth (Ruth 3:11), *"And now, my daughter, don't be afraid. I will do for you all you ask. All the people of my town know that you are a woman of noble character."* and, in Proverbs 12:4, *"A wife of noble character is her husband's crown, but a disgraceful wife is like decay in his bones."*

The original Hebrew word for virtuous is Chayil (khah' - yil). It means a force, an army, strength, able, substance, worthy, capable, strong, valiant. Whoa! What? I'm supposed to be strong and valiant, too? Yes, dear one, and you already are. God created you that way.

A Wife of Noble Character is a Virtuous Woman

A wife who is virtuous is able to take care of her home, is worthy, strong, serves and loves her husband, is capable and industrious. Most importantly, a virtuous wife is what her husband (not any other husband, but HER husband) needs. God created woman to be man's helper.

The Lord God said, "It is not good for the man to be alone. I will make a helper suitable for him." Genesis 2:18

What the ideal woman is for YOUR husband is as unique as he is; but while the specifics of how to be a suitable helper to your husband are unique to him and your marriage, the concept is the same - a wife of noble character is her husband's crown.

15

Learning your husband's love languages and serving him through those love languages is a great way to ensure that you are the Proverbs 31 wife that YOUR husband needs. My husband's love languages include gifts and acts of service. This is not saying that the only way to make him happy is to buy stuff for him. I will pick up his favorite snack at the grocery store or leave him a love note. Your husband may respond to words of affirmation or physical touch. The key is learning what your husband needs from his wife; this Proverbs 31 woman in his life.

We were created to be his helpmeet. What does your husband need in a modern Proverbs 31 woman? Have you asked him? I encourage you to pray about this and see what God reveals to you. Then, ask your husband what he needs from you. You may learn that what you thought was important to him is not and that there are other things that he would rather you do. Husbands are funny creatures. When I asked my husband this question, he told me how much he appreciates my making his homemade sweet tea. He says that it shows how much I care for him. Really? Who knew that something so small (in my eyes) touched him so much!

Bible Gateway has a great commentary on a wife of noble character. You may wish to check it out.

What makes your husband unique? How can you be a crown to him and not decay in his bones? What are three things that you know your husband would appreciate you doing that you don't already do or don't do very often?

If you aren't sure, spend some time this week asking God to reveal this to you.

Study Guide

Before reading this chapter, what were your thoughts on the Proverbs 31 woman?

How do you feel about the Proverbs 31 woman now?

What do you feel is the biggest challenge of the Proverbs 31 woman in today's world?

What is God telling you about this?

Write down any verses from Proverbs 31:10-31 that stand out to you.

> *Her husband has full confidence in her and lacks nothing of value.*
>
> **Proverbs 31:11**

Her Husband Has Full Confidence In Her, Does Yours?

Her husband has full confidence in her. At first read of Proverbs 31:10-31, it may be easy to overlook this verse.

In fact, the verse only indirectly mentions the Proverbs 31 woman. Instead, it tells us that her husband has full confidence in her (TRUSTS her) and lacks nothing of value. What an incredible testimony to the character of this godly woman!

Let's take a closer look at this verse. The ESV translation reads:

The heart of her husband trusts in her, And he will have no lack of gain.

Now let's examine some of the words from within the verse: (the information below is from Strong's Concordance)

Heart – Strong's 3820 – לב – leb = the heart; figuratively used widely for the feelings, the will, and even the intellect. Also translated mind, understanding, wisdom.

Trust – Strong's 982 – בטח – batach = to hasten toward refuge; figuratively to trust, be confident, be secure in, be sure. The KJV says "*doth safely trust in her*".

What do we see? A woman who evokes her husband's complete confidence in her, not only in the way she manages their home and raises their children, but in their relationship as well. She does not use her strengths and abilities to try to undermine him, but to strengthen the unity between them.

What does she do specifically to possess this trust?

Scripture gives a few details:

Verse 11 tells us he has no lack of gain. The NIV words it, "*he lacks nothing of value*". Perhaps, it is because of how well she manages their money, or because he is so content with their relationship that he has no desire to chase after anything else. At the very least, we see that he is content with their lifestyle as well as their relationship. What are some other ways that "Her Husband Has Full Confidence in Her"?

If asked, would your husband say that he has full confidence in you? In how you manage the home and raise the children? In how you steward the family budget? In how you speak to others? That he can count on you to do what you say you will do? If so, well done, my friend. You are a crown to your husband.

Most of us, however, come up short in at least one area. Although my husband assures me that he does trust me and he doesn't feel that he is lacking anything (He tells me that he has all he needs with God and me!), while studying this verse, God has, indeed, convicted me of something that I believe relates to my husband's confidence in me: how I handle stress.

Today was a rough day. I had website issues galore (Praise God they are fixed now!) and some work issues, too. I was stressed and short-tempered. I didn't lash out at my husband, but, instead, rebuffed his attempts to calm and comfort me. How can my husband have full confidence in me when he thinks he has to walk on eggshells around me? I am certainly not proud of this, but am kneeling before God in thanksgiving that He has made this known to me. I intend to focus on this weakness, pray about it and work hard to correct it. My husband deserves better and so does our Heavenly Father.

What about you? Her Husband Has Full Confidence In Her, Does Yours?

If you don't know, ask him. If you are aware of an area that you can improve - either because your husband has shared it with you or God has revealed it to you, ask God to shine a light on that area. Thank Him for revealing it to you and spend some time in prayer asking Him to help you change.

Study Guide

Does your husband have full confidence in you? Why or why not?

How can you improve in this area?

What is God whispering to you about this?

Use a concordance to find more about what the Bible says about any area that you are struggling in. Write the verses in your journal and pray over them.

She brings him good, not harm,

all the days of her life.

Proverbs 31:12

Do You Bring Him Good, Not Harm?

As we continue our discussion of what it means to be a Proverbs 31 woman in today's world, we make our way to verse 12.

What exactly does Proverbs 31:12 mean? The word "good", in this context, means considering your husband's happiness and well-being in everything you do. This noble woman builds her husband up instead of tearing him down.

She speaks kindly and doesn't continually nag and complain.

She cheerfully, yes, cheerfully, picks up his dirty laundry from the floor for the six hundredth time.

She does not complain about him to others (girlfriends included). Instead, she is to build him up and speak of his good traits to others. (If you are thinking that your husband doesn't have any good traits, I beg you to pray over this and consider Christian counseling. I have had women tell me that they can't think of anything positive to say about their husbands to which I answer that if they have nothing positive to say, don't say anything. Instead, they need to pray about what they are grateful for when it comes to their husbands. For example, does he provide a roof over her head? Is he active in the church? In most cases, wives tend to overlook the many things they can be thankful for in their husbands.)

She does not waste time scrolling on Facebook or playing games on her phone when her husband or children need her. (This is not saying that she should never do those things, but that her husband's needs should come before her own pleasure and game time).

She spends time in prayer and Bible study deepening her relationship with God and even learning more about how she can be a wife that is pleasing in God's eyes. (Joshua 1:8 ESV "*This Book of the Law shall not depart from your mouth, but you shall meditate on it day and night, so that you may be careful to do according to all* *that is written in it. For then you will make your way prosperous, and then you will have good success."* and Proverbs 31:30 *"Charm is deceptive, and beauty is fleeting; but a woman who fears the Lord is to be praised"*)

She submits to her husband and does not intentionally defy him. (Ephesians 5:22-24 ESV *"Wives, submit to your own husbands, as to the Lord. For the husband is the head of the wife even as Christ is the head of the church, his body, and is himself its Savior. Now as the church submits to Christ, so also wives should submit in everything to their husbands."*)

She looks for ways to be his helpmeet. This can be anything from making sure that he has his favorite beverage in the fridge to helping him in the yard. (Genesis 2:18 ESV *"Then the Lord God said, "It is not good that the man should be alone; I will make him a helper fit for him.""*)

She asks about his day and listens for his struggles so that she can better support him.

She does not rebuke his desire for sex with her. (1 Corinthians 7:4 ESV *For the wife does not have authority over her own body, but the husband does. Likewise the husband does not have authority over his own body, but the wife does.*)

She dresses modestly leaving "sexy" clothes for her husband's eyes only. (1 Timothy 2:9-10 ESV *"Likewise also that women should adorn themselves in respectable apparel, with modesty and self-control, not with braided* *hair and gold or pearls or costly attire, but with what is proper for women who profess godliness—with good works."*)

She keeps her home well-managed and clean, creating a sanctuary for her husband. (Luke 11:25 ESV *"And when it comes, it finds the house swept and put in order."*)

She strives to have a quiet and gentle spirit, providing a refuge for her husband instead of being harsh, vile, loud or rude. (1 Peter 3:4 *"but let your adorning be the hidden person of the heart with the imperishable beauty of a gentle and quiet spirit, which in God's sight is very precious."*)

Study Guide

In looking over the list above (and it is by no means exhaustive as there are always ways we can bring out husbands good, not harm), how do you do?

Are there areas you can improve on?

What things do you do well?

Proverbs 31:10-31 is written by a mother describing to her son what to look for in a wife. Would you give your son the same advice?

What additional advice would you give to your son in looking for a wife?

What other verses come to mind regarding bringing your husband good, not harm?

She selects wool and flax

and works with eager hands.

Proverbs 31:13

She Works With Willing Hands

During our examination of Proverbs 31:10-31, we have already learned the basics of what a Proverbs 31 woman is and how her husband has full confidence in her. We have also discussed the ways that the Proverbs 31 woman brings her husband good, not harm. Now, we will explore Proverbs 31:13.

It's not difficult to be discouraged or even overwhelmed when you read that this wife of noble character selects wool and flax (yes, she obtains raw material to sew clothes and cook meals!). In fact, she most likely did not buy the raw material, but rather, selected it from her own herd (wool) and fields (flax). In today's world, most of us do not have herds of sheep or fields of flax to obtain raw materials from. In fact, most of us, myself included, do not sew our own clothes or clothes for our families. To be honest, I am not sure that I could sew a button on and have it stay secure for more than a few minutes. If you do sew your own clothes, I am duly impressed and you are amazing, but there is still a lesson for you to learn here - just bear with me a bit.

Times have changed and that is okay, but I think the key words to consider in the scripture above are "*works with eager hands*". Some translations read "*willing hands*", instead of eager hands. The word willing comes from the Hebrew word אֲבֵה ה chephets (pronounced kay-fets) and means pleasure, desire, delight, purpose, matter or simply willing.

As women, as wives, we have responsibilities every day. The responsibilities vary by home and marriage, but can include cooking meals, doing laundry, grocery shopping, keeping a neat and clean home, caring for children, working outside the home, time in ministry, tending to the garden, pets or livestock, etc. Think of your responsibilities or duties each day. Are you doing them with "*willing hands*"? Or are you grumbling, complaining or doing them reluctantly?

Very few women that I have worked with or talked to love to do laundry or clean, many are vocal about how much they dislike those things. We all have one or two (or more) household responsibilities that we dread. What we need to remember, though, is that God has commanded us to do everything without complaining (Philippians 2:14 "*Do everything without complaining and arguing,*"). He also instructs us that in all we do, we are to do it for the glory of the Lord (1 Corinthians 10:31 ESV *So, whether you eat or drink, or whatever you do, do all to the glory of God.*)

If we are whining or resentful about our responsibilities (any of them!), are we glorifying God? Or, are we willfully disobeying Him?

I simply cannot stand to mop floors. I can't help it; I've never enjoyed that chore. It took me a long time to get to this point, but now, when I need to mop floors, I turn Pandora radio to Christian Contemporary music and get cracking. While I mop, I talk to God and thank him for the opportunity to clean for Him and my husband. It makes a chore that I dislike much more enjoyable. It is not the mopping that has changed, it is my heart. I now mop the floors with willing hands.

What is one chore that you find yourself complaining about doing? How can you change your heart to perform that chore with willing hands? If you aren't sure, spend some time in prayer asking God to reveal to you how you can have a change of heart.

How do you feel about the responsibilities you have in the home and family? Are you doing them with willing hands and an eager heart?

Study Guide

What is one chore that you find yourself complaining about doing?

How can you change your heart to perform that chore with willing hands?

How do you feel about the responsibilities you have in the home and with your family?

Are you performing those responsibilities with willing hands and an eager heart?

Pray for God to reveal to you any changes you need to make in this area.

She is like the merchant ships,

bringing her food from afar.

Proverbs 31:14

How a Godly Wife is like a Merchant Ship and the Amazing Benefits of Homemade Food

Merchant ships and a godly wife? What? How can those two even be in the same sentence? Seems crazy, right, but bear with me, friends. In Proverbs 31 verse 14, we read, "*She is like the merchant ships, bringing her food from afar.*"

We know that for hundreds, or even thousands, of years, merchant ships brought food from other countries. Even today, most countries import food from around the world and much of it arrives on merchant ships. In our homes, however, we bring our food from the supermarket or, sometimes even our own gardens. In most cases (of course, not all), the wife does the food shopping. Some wives go from market to market looking for the best deal or best items; others, like me, choose to shop at only one place for convenience. We also have a very large garden and preserve our vegetables each year.

In Biblical times and even just a few decades ago, most food was not prepared when bought. The flax was ground, the dough was kneaded and the bread baked. Today, with much of what we buy, all of that has been done for us. Does that mean that because we buy store-bought instead of homemade that we are not godly wives? Absolutely not, but let's look at the benefits of homemade versus pre-prepared:

Homemade food is fresher and not loaded with preservatives that must be added to already prepared food to allow for a longer shelf life

Homemade is more natural and healthy (see above but the ingredients themselves tend to be healthier, as well)

Similar to healthier, homemade food does not have the high sodium content that store canned and frozen food has.

Homemade is cheaper, in most cases, than store-prepared and purchased.

You can add love as an ingredient to homemade food. Sounds cheesy, but if you make a casserole, by hand, as opposed to heating up a frozen dinner, which do you think shows that you went the extra mile to show love to your husband and family?

Homemade does not always mean that it takes longer to make.

Please don't mistake what I am saying here. I am not saying that by buying prepared foods you are not a wife of noble character or are a bad wife. There are always times that buying prepared makes sense - I do it, too (For example, I don't bake my own bread. I always say I will, but I don't). What I'm saying is that there are many benefits to making homemade food.

So, how are you supposed to fit in making homemade foods? Well, many homemade foods don't really take much longer (if at all) to make than store bought. You can also set aside time one night per week to cook in batches or once a month on a Saturday or Sunday after church. You will love the taste and the savings, as well as your husband's appreciation!

Another way that you can be like merchant ships is by meal planning and preparation. On my blog, I share the basics of meal planning. By meal planning and preparation, you will save money (less than takeout), time and stress. Adding meal planning was the single thing that made our home run smoother and saved me time, money and headaches. I wholeheartedly recommend it.

Finally, by having staple ingredients in your pantry, you can more easily meal plan and create quick, homemade meals without a last minute run to the supermarket. Here is a list of the items that I always have on hand, ensuring that I can create a meal in a pinch. Even I occasionally get behind in meal planning or can't get to the store for one reason or another (weather, car troubles, tight budgets, illness, etc.)

Refrigerator:

- Vegetables - we can from our garden, but sometimes we run out or need things that we don't grow. Our favorites are tomatoes, cucumbers, lettuce, a variety of peppers and carrots.

- Fruit - bananas, apples, oranges and berries

- Eggs - we are fortunate to have nearly 30 chickens to provide us fresh eggs year round

- Whole milk

- Deli meat (turkey, chicken and ham - I alternate)

- Yogurt

- Fresh garlic bulbs

Freezer:

- Variety of organic, frozen vegetables (e.g., broccoli, green beans, corn, mixed vegetables, carrots)

- variety of fish (salmon and tilapia mostly)

- Chicken - breasts, parts and whole chickens

- Ground beef

- Whole beef (I look for what is on sale)

- Pork (we buy a hog each year for about $150. The meat lasts us for about 9 months, sometimes more - except bacon - we go through a lot of bacon!)

- Various cheeses (shredded, block and sliced. we always have cheddar and mozzarella, but will buy others as they are on sale)

Pantry:

- Crackers (saltines, graham, Ritz)

- Canned beans (black beans, navy beans, garbanzo, and pinto beans)

- Seasonings (basil, oregano; garlic, onion, salt – table and kosher, pepper, dill weed, thyme, etc.)

- White bread and whole grain bread (my husband prefers white, I prefer whole grain)

- Naan bread (for making homemade pizzas)

- Rice (white, basmati, jasmine, long grain)

- Pasta (varieties)

- Some chips (usually Cape Cod chips)

- Peanut butter

- Local honey

- Tortillas (for tacos, burritos and breakfast burritos)

- Olive oil

- Cereal and oatmeal

- Vinegar (red, white, balsamic and rice)

- Vegetable oil

- Flour

- Sugar

- Corn starch

- Beef, chicken, and vegetable stock

Of course, this is not an exhaustive list of my pantry and refrigerator, but I always have these items on hand. With them, I am prepared to create a homemade meal without a trip to the store. (I happen to live twenty minutes from the grocery store. Certainly not convenient if I forget an ingredient!). I am always looking for new ways to be a godly wife (or like merchant ships!)

There are many verses in the Bible about storing food for the future; I like to remind myself of these as I food shop and plan meals for my husband. Here are some of my favorites:

Genesis 41:35

"Then let them gather all the food of these good years that are coming, and store up the grain for food in the cities under Pharaoh's authority, and let them guard it."

Luke 12:19

'And I will say to my soul, "Soul, you have many goods laid up for many years to come; take your ease, eat, drink and be merry."'

Proverbs 3:10

So your barns will be filled with plenty And your vats will overflow with new wine.

Study Guide

How are you like a merchant ship?

Do you meal-plan? Why or why not?

Do you prepare more homemade foods than store bought?

What is God telling you about this verse?

She gets up while it is still night;

she provides food for her family and portions for her

female servants.

Proverbs 31:15

How to Go From a Night Owl to a Morning Glory

If you had asked me ten years ago if I was a morning person or a night owl, I would not have hesitated and said easily "a night owl". I loved to stay up after everyone else went to bed and have some "me time". Time watching TV or in my art studio, time to just be. As I have evolved as a wife and even as a mother, and have put my focus on being a Proverbs 31 wife, I have found that going to bed earlier and getting up earlier has made a huge difference in how my home runs and, in my marriage. Now, I am usually in bed by 10pm or so and up at 6am. As much as I resisted this change, it has made my days more productive and has blessed me in numerous ways.

Let's look at Proverbs 31:15 and what it says about the Proverbs 31 woman rising early:

If we look at Strong's concordance, we see some further explanation on this verse and the meanings within it.

Rises – Strong's 6965 – קוּם – quwm = to arise, to stand, to be set, to fulfill, to establish, to endure, to stir up, to carry out. Often used with a sense of rising in preparation or rising in power.

Quwm does not refer to getting out of bed, which is an entirely different word in Hebrew (shakam). It refers to rising up with a plan and a purpose. This is what we see the wife of noble character doing.

The first two items on her daily agenda are to feed to her household and attend to her servants.

1. Gives food to her household – We have already seen in verse 14 that she is diligent in selecting and purchasing

37

choice foods for her household. Here we see that she supervises the meals as well. Does she cook them herself? We don't know. The passage does not tell us that. What we do see is that she pays attention to all aspects of feeding her family.

2. Gives portions to her servants (or maidens as is found in some translations) – Two words are of interest here: portions and maidens.

Portions – Strong's 2706 – חק – choq = an appointment of time, space, quantity, labor or usage. Commandment, custom, decree, prescribed task

Maiden -Strong's 5291 – נערה – na`arah = girl (from infancy through adolescence), young woman, marriageable young woman, maid, female attendant, female servant.

Proverbs 31:15 in Today's World

Okay, okay. I can hear you groaning and see you rolling your eyes. Servants? Who has servants? We know from the text that the Proverbs 31 woman is well-off, so yes, she probably has servants, but here's what I want you to focus on: She gets up early and has a plan for her day. Do you?

We probably don't have servants, but each of us has a list of things to do in our lives that is most likely an arm's-length long. In any given day, we might need to:

- Wash, dry and fold the laundry
- Cook the family's meals
- Run the dog to the vet
- Dust the living room

- Run the vacuum
- Wash the dishes
- and on and on and on

Our to-do list may look a bit different than the one of the woman described in Proverbs 31:15, but this woman gets up early and has a plan in place to get it all done. One of the best ways that I have found to make a plan and have a more productive day is to establish routines in the morning and evening. You can read more about that on my website.

We can't take a trip without an itinerary or map, so why navigate through life without one? Routines can help you navigate through your days and make your days (and home!) run more smoothly.

Proverbs 31:15 - Rising Early

So, we have established that to be more like the woman in Proverbs 31:15, we need to make a plan for our day, but what about this getting up while it is still dark business? I know, dear friend, that this can be a tough one, especially if you are naturally a night owl. Here are a few tips to help you get up earlier without compromising much needed rest:

1. Don't hit the snooze button.

Hitting your alarm's snooze button does not give you more of the restful REM sleep. Your body and mind are not recuperating; no, you are just wasting time. Personally, I noticed that regularly hitting snooze made my thinking even cloudier when the alarm went off. Your mind starts to ignore the alarm bells.

2. Wake up at the same time every day.

Your body becomes conditioned to this and regulates your sleep patterns accordingly. You get more of that precious REM sleep and when you have a regular wake time; your body actually begins the process of waking up long before your alarm sounds.

3. Create Some Accountability

Partner with a friend to keep you both accountable. Agree to text or call each other when you wake up. Years ago, I met a friend at the gym at 6:30 am. I knew that if I didn't get up on time, I was letting her down, too.

4. Start Small

If you normally go to bed at midnight, shoot for 11:45 pm for the first few days of this change. Then go to 11:30 pm, etc. Do the same thing in the morning. (If you normally get up at 8:00 am, set the alarm for 7:45 am). Keep it going until you get to the sleep and wake time that you are working towards.

5. Pay attention to what you eat and drink.

I used to be able to drink coffee at bedtime and have no problem falling asleep. Now, drinking coffee after 2 pm prevents me from falling or staying asleep. Are you drinking caffeinated beverages? Perhaps, stop drinking them earlier in the day. In addition, eating food that is good for you (as opposed to processed, fried or other heavy foods), is better for your body and will help you sleep better, as well.

6. Develop the Right Attitude

Get excited about your day and you will jump out of bed. Don't drive yourself with guilt about why you have to be rising early. Make waking up early something you get to do. Of course, the joy of serving your family can drive you. Don't be afraid to motivate yourself by doing something fun in the morning. Exercise, spend time in God's Word or time with a hobby that you enjoy. Even better, think of the benefits that your husband and family will receive from you getting up early. You can also keep track of your progress and reward yourself when you reach a milestone of getting up early for so many days or weeks in a row.

Study Guide

What steps can you take to get up earlier?

What steps can you take to have a plan for your day?

Do you already get up early? If so, what benefits have you enjoyed because you do?

Use a concordance to look up verses on time management and productivity. Journal about any that stand out to you.

She considers a field and buys it;

out of her earnings she plants a vineyard.

Proverbs 31:16

The Proverbs 31 Woman is Savvy and Skilled

In this biblical narrative of the "ideal" Christian wife, we read about how she manages her time, her home and even how her husband reveres her. When I first studied the Proverbs 31 woman, I was struck by verse 16: "*She considers a field and buys it; out of her earnings she plants a vineyard*". Not only is her home impeccable, she takes care of herself and is organized, but she buys fields, plants vineyards and sells her handmade goods! That's quite the standard to live up to. While I would agree that this virtuous wife is a female entrepreneur, it is these verses, which we will talk about in future sections of this book, that seem to indicate she is a savvy business woman:

"*She sees that her trading is profitable, and her lamp does not go out at night.*" (Prov. 31:18)

"*She makes linen garments and sells them, and supplies the merchants with sashes.*" (Prov.31:24)

In verse 16, one could argue that this is another example of her female entrepreneur skills and experience; I think it goes deeper than that. Let's take a closer look at this verse.

The first part of this verse illustrates that she makes decisions carefully "*she considers*". In other words, she does not make rash decisions. In this case, she thoughtfully (and most likely prayerfully) evaluated the land and decided that it was a good decision to buy it. The location may have been excellent, the land rich and the price right. While we don't know her exact reasons for determining that the field was a good purchase, we do know that she "considers" it first.

The next key to learning more about the Proverbs 31 woman is that she made the purchase "*out of her earnings*". Most likely, these earnings were from the sale of the linen garments mentioned in verse 24. She didn't take out a loan or ask her husband for money (although I am certain that, since he is the head of household, she discussed the purchase with him, first), but rather purchased the land with her own earnings.

Finally, "*she plants a vineyard*". She does not restrict herself and her family to the bare necessities of life; she is able to enjoy some comforts, as well... She plants a vineyard, for which the yield of grapes may be used for wine, medicine, or sacrifice. Planting a vineyard is hard physical work. We don't know from this text, however, if she physically planted it or used household labor to do the planting. In Gill's Exposition of the Entire Bible, we do glean some context:

"And it is observable, that in the Hebrew text there is a double reading; the "Keri", or marginal reading, is feminine; but the "Cetib", or writing, is masculine; to show that she did it by means of men, she made use of in her vineyard for that service; it being, as Aben Ezra observes, not the custom and business of women to plant vineyards, but men. It may be rendered, "he planted", and be applied to her husband, Christ; who, through the ministry of the word in his church, plants souls in it; and happy are they who are the planting of the Lord! trees of righteousness, that he may be glorified, Isaiah 61:3."

Study Guide

With deeper study of Proverbs 31:16, this verse shows me that while she may have been an entrepreneur, she makes judicious decisions, is financially responsible and industrious. Would you agree or disagree? Why?

Do you make good decisions for your family – financial, relational and practical?

What can you do to improve?

What is God telling you about this verse and how to apply it to your life?

She sets about her work vigorously;

her arms are strong for her tasks.

Proverbs 31:17

How to Find Strength as a Proverbs 31 Woman

Strength as a Proverbs 31 woman. Let's take a look at Proverbs 31:17 and what it means to have strength as a woman of noble character.

I have an NIV Bible and find that it is a bit easier to understand than some of the other versions, but for this verse, I think it is important to look at other translations to really understand this Proverbs 31 woman. We'll examine this verse in depth for the key words in this short, but meaty verse.

Proverbs 31:17 (NIV)

She sets about her work vigorously;

her arms are strong for her tasks.

Proverbs 31:17 (NKJV)

She girds herself with strength,And strengthens her arms.

Proverbs 31:17 (KJV)

She girdeth her loins with strength, and strengtheneth her arms.

A Proverbs 31 wife knows how to prepare for her work.. The Hebrew phrase for "she girds her loins" means to prepare oneself for something requiring readiness, strength, or endurance.

The original Hebrew words and meanings for strength and strong are:

Strength: 'owz' (oze) - force, security, majesty, praise:- boldness, loud, power

Strong: 'amats' (aw-mats') - to be alert, steadfastedly minded, prevail

Therefore, this is saying that she prepares herself with loud, powerful and bold praise. She is strong and knows who she is. She is a child of the King and she knows it!

How do you "gird your loins" for your day or work? For me, I spend my first thirty minutes of the day reading a devotional, writing scripture in my journal and doing a daily Bible Study. Starting my day in His Word, helps me to keep my focus on Him throughout my day. It is the greatest way to "gird my loins" and prepare me for the day ahead.

The next key phrase in this verse is "*strengthens her arms*". The Proverbs 31 woman needs to be strong and have endurance to get through her busy days. I do not believe that this verse is telling us that we have to lift weights to have strong arms, but by the hard work she puts in daily, she is strengthened. In biblical times, women were not going to spin class! Rather, they were strengthened by the hard work of their daily tasks.

In present day, we have so many conveniences that make our tasks less physically demanding, but it is no less important today, to keep our strength up.

We are to take care of the body that God gave us while on earth. Eating right, exercising, and getting enough rest. If we are not caring for our bodies, we will not have the strength to manage everything we need to accomplish. Women are busy! We are taking care of children, cleaning, cooking, laundry, errands, caring for our husbands. If we are not caring for ourselves, how can we have the strength and endurance to care for others?

I am not saying that you have to go to the gym or avoid cupcakes to be a Proverbs 31 woman. What I am saying is that by taking care of our own bodies, we are better able to handle our ever-growing to-do list. A sluggish, unhealthy woman is less likely to feel strength and feel power (as in the scripture above) than one who is well-rested and cares for her body.

In full disclosure here: I need to lose about fifty pounds and rarely go a day without eating chocolate. I am a cancer survivor so I have not always been healthy. I know that by exercising and saying no to Reese's Peanut Butter Cups I might be able to shed the extra weight and better care for my body. It is a struggle. There is no judgement here. I know that God is shining a light on this verse for me for a reason.

(If you do not have a concordance or access to Bible commentaries, BibleHub is a good online resource.)

Study Guide

How do you strengthen your arms for your work?

What steps can you take to improve your spiritual strength?

What steps can you take to improve your physical strength?

What is God telling you about this verse and how it applies to your life?

She sees that her trading is profitable,

and her lamp does not go out at night.

Proverbs 31:18

Her Lamp Does Not Go Out At Night

Does this woman ever sleep? First, we read that she gets up early, now we read that her lamp does not go out at night. Wait. What? That was my reaction to this verse. I can barely function on eight hours sleep, now Proverbs 31:18 tells us that she is up all night, too? Well, not so fast. In deeper study of this verse, we learn much more about this woman who is above rubies.

Let's look at both parts to this verse:

She sees that her trading is profitable.

Many will point to this verse to indicate that the Proverbs 31 woman was an entrepreneur. We talked a bit about that in an earlier chapter. While she may very well have been an entrepreneur, let's look a little deeper to get at the meaning of this part of the verse. Many verses in the Bible use allegories or stories to illustrate Biblical truths. Upon further study of this verse, I believe that this, indeed, is one of those illustrations.

In Gill's Exposition of the Bible (note that this is from the King James Version), he writes:

"She perceiveth that her merchandise is good,…. That it turns to good account; that her trading to heaven is of great advantage; that she grows rich hereby; that her merchandise with Wisdom, or Christ, is better than the merchandise of silver, and the gain thereby than fine gold; and though her voyages are attended with trouble and danger, yet are profitable, and therefore she is not discouraged, but determined to pursue them; she is like the merchant man, seeking goodly pearls, who finds a pearl of great price, worth all his trouble"

According to Gill, her merchandise is what she is doing with her time on earth in exchange for our riches we are promised in heaven!

Another exposition, Matthew Poole's English Annotations of the Bible says "she finds great comfort and good success in her labours."

Wheedon's Commentary on the Bible explains it this way: " Valuable, profitable, and highly appreciated, and this makes her all the more industrious; so that sometimes, at least, she works at it all night in order to supply the great demand for her goods."

We are called to examine our lives and ensure that we are living in faith striving to walk more like Him every day. If you "examined" your merchandise, are you living a life pleasing to God? A life that you can find comfort in knowing that you are inheriting the riches of the Kingdom?

Let's look at the second part of the verse.

"…and her lamp does not go out at night."

Another look at Gill's Exposition and we find:

"...her candle goeth not out by night; her lamp of profession, which is always kept burning, or the glorious light of the Gospel, which always continues in the darkest times the church ever has been in; or her spiritual prosperity, which, though it may be damped, will never be extinct; when the candle of the wicked is often put out, Job 21:17; It may denote her diligence in working; who, as she rises early in the morning, Proverbs 31:15, so sits up late at night, and is never weary of well doing, night and day" (Gill's Exposition).

And Poole's:

Her candle goeth not out by night; which is not to be taken strictly, but only signifies her unwearied care and industry, which is oft expressed by labouring day and night, or continually.

So it seems that the candle or lamp illustrates that she is unwavering in her commitment to serving her family and God. She does work hard, often into the night, but it is the light of the plan of salvation that keeps her going.

We have hope that the Living God is on the throne. It is through our overworked and overwhelmed days that we can press on. No matter how difficult the season of your life. No matter how many things on your to-do list. No matter how many spills that you have cleaned up or dishes you have done or laundry still to do, God is still in control. We have a promise in Him. We are called to be salt and light on this earth. How can we be the salt and light and if we are stressed, worried, frazzled and not keeping our eyes on the Father? When we cast our fears and doubt aside, we can live in the truth of His promises and share that truth with others.

For I know the plans I have for you," declares the LORD, "plans to prosper you and not to harm you, plans to give you hope and a future. Jeremiah 29:11

Study Guide

What can you do today to live a life pleasing to Him and the promises we have in Him?

What can you put into practice today to ensure that your lamp does not go out at night?

If you examined your life, would you say that you are living a life pleasing to God? Why or why not?

What do you think needs to change?

In her hand she holds the distaff

and grasps the spindle with her fingers.

Proverbs 31:19

Do You Need to Know How to Sew to Be a Woman of Noble Character?

This verse is one that some women glance over and move on because the tools mentioned are not those commonly used in our modern society. Distaff and spindle. Biblehub explains what these items are: "Till comparatively recent times the sole spinning implements were the spindle and distaff. The spindle, which is the fundamental apparatus in all spinning, was nothing more nor less than a round stick or rod of wood, about 12 inches in length, tapering towards each extremity, and having at its upper end a notch or slit, into which the yarn might be caught or fixed. In general, a ring or whorl of stone or clay was passed round the upper part of the spindle to give it momentum and steadiness when in rotation. The distaff or rod was a rather longer and stronger bar or stick, around one end of which, in a loose coil or ball, the fibrous material to be spun was wound. The other extremity of the distaff was carried under the left arm, or fixed in the girdle at the left side, so as to have the coil of flax in a convenient position for drawing out to yarn."

A Wife of Noble Character in Biblical Times

I will admit, these are not tools that are commonly (if ever) used today, but it is important to look at them to understand that spinning yarn was hard work on the hands. As we have learned, the Proverbs 31 woman is not afraid of hard work and often, her hands take a beating. Hands are mentioned throughout the Bible and (I have written many posts on my blog on Bible symbolism, including one on hands in the Bible), but take note that hardworking hands are not enough.

A woman needs to be skillful at her tasks. In biblical times, God prepared women to be skilled in spinning the various fabrics for the complex decorating of the tabernacle (ref. Ex. 35:25-26). The English language originally called such skillful women spinsters, though that name now has very different connotations. A woman must know how to do domestic and other hand tasks skillfully in order to be a virtuous wife.

The virtuous woman of Proverbs 31 was a very competent woman at many levels. She bought and managed commercial real estate and manufacturing businesses to help build the family estate (Prov. 31:16, 24), and she could spin thread from raw materials. She could take a spinning wheel and loom and teach maidens how to make cloth perfectly (Prov. 31:15). She could do the work herself, show how it should be done, and teach others.

The Modern Day Wife of Noble Character

The modern day wife of noble character does not spin cloth to make clothes. It would be a waste of her skills and time. She can buy clothes at the mall (or online!) that are made well and not terribly expensive. She makes better use of her time by learning other skills (mending, cooking, knowledge in her profession, etc.) and using her earnings to buy the clothes and other household items that she needs. However, when the situation calls for it or out of necessity, she can "do it from scratch," whether in the closet or the kitchen. When she needs to, she can make cakes not from a boxed mix (although, sometimes, it's the way to go!) and can cook to satisfy her husband and family. (Gen 18:6; 27:9). This is a woman worth more than rubies!

THE COMPLETE PROVERBS 31 WOMAN

What should a woman learn to do skillfully today? Plan and prepare good meals for your husband and family. Learn to use or improve your computer skills for research, when needed... Know first aid and how to mend clothing. (This is one that I honestly am terrible about!) Plan her days and weeks to be productive. Communicate effectively with her husband, co-workers and fellow church congregants. Know where and how to buy food and household items at the best prices. Balance her checkbooks. Decorate a house for appeal, comfort, and investment. Find and use the best appliances and tools inside and outside the house.

This is the perfect woman, as described by a mother for her son (Prov. 31:1-2,10). She fears the LORD with all her heart (Prov. 31:30). Her husband can trust in her completely, because she will do him good and right every day of her life (Prov. 31:11-12). After these two priorities, she is a diligent worker to provide for her family, her home, and build the family estate in any way she can. She is diligent and skillful in the use of her hands.

Study Guide

What do your hands do in the course of your day?

What skills do you believe that a wife of noble character in today's world needs to be successful?

55

What skills would you like to learn?

Where can you learn these skills?

What is God telling you about this verse and how it applies to your life?

She opens her arms to the poor

and extends her hands to the needy.

Proverbs 31:20

Extend Your Hands to the Needy

When we read Proverbs 31, much of the attributes of this ideal woman are related to her managing her home, her finances and caring for her family and servants. Proverbs 31:20, however, shows us that she is not just home centric, but loves her neighbor, as well.

She opens her arms to the poor and extends her hands to the needy. - Proverbs 31:20

God has created women to be compassionate. We are the nurturers.

On my website, I shared about using our hands to hold on to things: our time, our money, our love. The Proverbs 31 woman is the opposite. She opens her arms to the poor and extends her hands to the needy. She is not holding on tightly to what is rightfully hers. She is sharing the fruits of her labor with those in need. Her charity does not end with a kind word or a promise to pray for others; it is more than a passive activity. Her helping may involve physical giving - food, clothing, other goods or it may include giving spiritual food to those who are poor in spirit, spiritually poor and needy, and who hunger and thirst after righteousness.

It's easy to be so wrapped up in our own lives and problems that focus just on what needs to get accomplished for our homes and families. God commands us, however, to help others and to love our neighbors. There are dozens, maybe hundreds of verses that point to the importance of helping others.

Proverbs 19:17 *Whoever is generous to the poor lends to the Lord, and he will repay him for his deed.*

Galatians 6:2 *Bear one another's burdens, and so fulfill the law of Christ.*

Deuteronomy 15:11 *For there will never cease to be poor in the land. Therefore I command you, 'You shall open wide your hand to your brother, to the needy and to the poor, in your land.'*

Think about your own family or circle of friends, perhaps your church community. Who comes to mind when you think of someone living out this verse? Is the woman who always provides a meal for the sick or shut-in? Or the one who tirelessly serves food at a local Soup Kitchen. Maybe it is the one that collects coats for children in shelters or the one who fosters at-risk youth or children in her home.

There are thousands of ways that we can live out this verse in our lives and how you can extend your hands to the needy. While some require giving of our own financial or physical resources, many won't cost anything but time and heart.

I encourage you today to look at your own life and examine how you are extending your hands to the needy. Are you giving only when it is convenient or do you truly have a heart to help those less fortunate? What is God asking of you? Have you prayed to Him to reveal to you how He would have you serve?

Here are some suggestions for ministering to others in your community:

- Participate in Operation Shoebox
- Participate in or spearhead a clothing drive
- Host a garage sale and donate the profits to a ministry or local charitable organization
- Instead of selling unused or unwanted items in your home, seek out donation centers where your no longer wanted items would be a blessing to someone in need
- Prepare a meal for an elderly person in your home, bring it to them and sit with them while they eat it.

Your companionship may do more for their spirit than the food could do for their bodies.

- Volunteer at a shelter or soup kitchen
- Consider fostering a child in your home (in the county that our church resides, there is only ONE foster family, but many children in need).
- Prepare a few "Blessing Bags" to keep in your car. Give them to the homeless that you encounter. You have no idea how much that simple gesture will affect another.
- Get involved in a ministry with a mission to serve others. At our church, my heart is for the Bethesda Ministry for single women, widows and orphans.
- In addition to your tithe, consider giving money to other ministries to support the needy. Church budgets are often tight and your extra few dollars could be a huge blessing to others. God will multiply your offering!

Study Guide

What do you do now to extend your hands to the needy?

What other things can you do to share the love of Christ and extend your hands to the needy?

Do you think you can give more financially? Physically?

When it snows, she has no fear for her household;

for all of them are clothed in scarlet.

Proverbs 31:21

Clothe Your Family in Scarlet - 6 Tips for Raising a Family of Faith

Brrr! This past winter has been bitter cold here in North Central Missouri. Much of the US has had frigid temperatures, snow and ice this winter. Proverbs 31:21 tells us that the virtuous woman is not afraid of cold weather. She has prepared her house (and its occupants) for the cold. If we have a fireplace, we have wood ready.

We buy rock salt and shovels to clear the walkways. We make sure that there are pairs of gloves and that scarves and hats are in good condition. (In my house, we have a tendency to lose gloves. I am always checking for pairs and buying more!) We cook warm and hearty meals, like soups and stews, this time of year. We prepare physically for the winter, but do we prepare spiritually?

Proverbs 31 not only addresses preparing our home and family for the cold weather, but it has a spiritual application. The term "clothed with scarlet" refers to the scarlet wool used by Moses in the Old Testament. It represents the blood that Jesus shed for the cleansing of sins for all humanity. Therefore, when we are "clothed in scarlet", we are covered by the blood of Jesus; we have been saved by His dying on the cross for our sins. The virtuous woman prepared for a spiritual winter by seeing that her family is clothed in scarlet – in which they are saved by faith. In this way, they will not fear any cold or dark time of trial. God will see us through it.

How to clothe your family in scarlet:

Start a new habit with your family this week to better clothe them in scarlet. Here are some ideas:

*If you don't already, pray before each meal, as a family

*Do a family devotional

There are great free devotional resources including:

 http://www.josh.org/resources/daily-devotional/todays-familydevotional/

http://www.truthforkids.com/kids-devotions-online/#.Uuf4jxDnbIU

http://www.focusonthefamily.com/parenting/spiritual_growth_for_kids/family_mealtime_devotionals.aspx

* Pray with your children (and spouse) at bedtime

* Let your family hear you talking to God, praying and/or reading the Bible

* Make a blessings jar – have each family member write down something they are thankful to God for (daily, weekly, whatever works for you) and then put it in the jar. Periodically review all of God's blessings in your life.

* Make God a regular topic of your conversations

Study Guide

How do you clothe your family in scarlet?

What can you do, this week, to build your family's faith?

Tie a piece of red yarn or ribbon around an item that you see throughout your day to remind you to "clothe your family in scarlet".

What is God telling you about how to apply this verse to
your life?

She makes coverings for her bed;

she is clothed in fine linen and purple.

Proverbs 31:22

She is Clothed in Fine Linen and Purple

If Pinterest were around in biblical times, this woman of
noble character would certainly be a "Pinterest-worthy"
wife! She is quite the accomplished seamstress, it seems.
But, dear friends, she is so much more than just that.

Strong's commentary on the Bible gives us some context
on the words used in this verse:

Makes – Strong's 6213 – עשה – asah = to do, fashion, accomplish, make

Coverings – Strong's 4765 – מרבד – marbad = [from the verb rabad (Strong's 7234) meaning to spread], spread (as in bedspread), coverlet.

As we look at this verse, it is important to consider the verse that comes before it.

She is not afraid of the snow for her household, for all her household are clothed with scarlet. Prov. 31:21

When we look at that verse, with this one, we might assume that the coverings for her bed are part of her preparedness for winter or hard times.

While we know that she makes the coverings, we are not given clues to how she makes them or exactly what those coverings are.   Although the King James Version translates 'marbad' as "coverings of tapestry" both here and in Prov. 7:16, the Hebrew word itself does not necessarily imply this. It is interesting to note that a derivative of this word is used to describe God's own works of creation as well as the miracles He performed on Israel's behalf. From that, we catch the idea of the creative process involved.

The Proverbs 31 woman's clothing reflects her character. She, of course, ensures that her family's needs are met, as well as that of the rest of her household (in biblical times, this could include house help or servants). But she also takes care of her own appearance. She is classy and takes the time to sew herself clothing of fine linen and purple - without being showy.

Keep in mind, she couldn't just run to the mall to buy a purple dress. She would have had to sew her own clothing.

Notice, though, that in Proverbs 31, the focus first is on how she takes care of her family and household. Only then does she worry about what she wears. This care and compassion for her family is one of the many attributes that make her beautiful. It is inward beauty.

Not to say that she can't look nice or care about her appearance, but as we are reminded in 1 Peter:

"Your beauty should not come from outward adornment, such as elaborate hairstyles and the wearing of gold jewelry or fine clothes. Rather, it should be that of your inner self, the unfading beauty of a gentle and quiet spirit, which is of great worth in God's sight." - 1 Peter 3:3-4

Our beauty comes from within. Our inner self. Who we are. How we show God's love to others. Not from the clothes we wear, the makeup we apply or the jewelry we add to accessorize.

The world, however, tells us something different. It tells us that we need to keep up with trends and always look fashionable. The Bible, however, reminds us that our beauty comes from within.

It's perfectly OK to take care of yourself and look good, but when it becomes an idol, it becomes sin.

So we know that the Proverbs 31 woman sewed her family's clothing and linens. She knew that how she took care of her home reflected on her, her husband and her family.

In historical context, we can assume that the cloth for the coverings was woven and then sewn. We have already seen the Proverbs 31 Woman as a hand-spinner, but besides the added "tapestry" in the King James translation, no weaving terms are used in the passage. We don't know if she wove the cloth herself, or had someone else do it.

The second half of this verse mentions coverings of a different kind.

Clothing – Strong's 3830 – לבש or לבוש – lebush' = clothing, garment, apparel, raiment

Fine linen – Strong's 8336 – ששי or שש – shesh or shaysh = something bleached white, linen, fine linen, marble, silk. Translated only once (Prov. 31:22) as "silk" in the KJV.

Purple – Strong's 713 – ארגמן – 'argaman = purple, red-purple (either the color or the dyed goods). Due to its cost, it is associated with royalty or the favor of royalty, nobility, the priests, and the temple.

In Proverbs 31, the words "clothing" and "clothed" are used both literally, this verse, and symbolically (verse 25). According to The Blue Letter Bible, the word 'lebuwsh' implies more than just articles of clothing. It also assumes that clothing reveals something about the wearer rank, status, or circumstance. In today's world, we still see evidence of that, although not as overt as in biblical times. As a child, we are taught, "don't judge a book by its cover"; however, as humans, we know that how we look does make an impression on others.

How we present ourselves to the world affects us both internally (as self-esteem and self-respect) and externally (how others view us). When we, as Christian women, wear clothing that is in conflict with our Christian values (revealing clothing, shirts with worldly or inappropriate text), we are sending a message about ourselves to others. We are ambassadors of Christ. As ambassadors, we need to dress the part. Don't we want others to see Christ when they see us?

We should not be wearing clothing that calls attention to our bodies and ourselves but should dress appropriately to honor God.

The Proverbs 31 Woman was not showy with her appearance and wealth, but modest and generous. She understood both her role as wife and woman in her family and society. She, of course, took care with her appearance, but her true beauty, and what she is "clothed" in, is found in a later verse: Proverbs 31:25.

Strength and dignity are her clothing, and she smiles at the future. Prov. 31:25

How are you "dressed", my friend? Are you presenting yourself as a daughter of The King or as a woman of this world?

Does your family come first? Do you take care of their needs, feed them, love others as Jesus loves us?

Study Guide

How are you "dressed"?

Are you presenting yourself as a daughter of The King or as a woman of this world?

What changes can you make today to dress, internally and externally as the daughter of The King?

What is God telling you about applying this verse to your life?

Her husband is respected at the city gate,

where he takes his seat among the elders of the land.

Proverbs 31:23

Her Husband is Respected at the City Gate

Her Husband is Respected at the City Gate. A seemingly innocuous verse, which does not directly mention the Proverbs 31 woman. In Ellicott's Commentary for English Readers, the author explains this verse in this way "Her husband is known in the gates. Instead of being a hindrance to her husband's advancement, she furthers it. Her influence for good extends to him also. Having no domestic anxieties, he is set free to do his part in public life."

This, in my opinion, is epic. The role of the wife of noble character, in many ways, is summed up in this verse. When a husband does not have to worry about his wife, her conduct, how his home is being managed or the children, he can be free to focus his mind on his work and ministries. Her husband is respected at the city gate.

One measure of a biblical wife is the reputation of her husband. Of course, her role is only one part of his reputation, but for the purposes of this book and our readers, I am just going to focus on her role in his reputation.

Others, especially your husband's friends, co-workers and church members, will respect him for his blessing of such a treasured wife and wisdom in marrying such a woman. As God intended in Eden, a woman can help a man in most every area of his life. We were created to be his "helpmeet".

Let's take a closer look at the word helpmeet. In God's Word to Women, we see the Hebrew words for help and meet.

HELP

Strong's # 5828 (Hebrew = ezer) aid: -- help

Strong's Root = # 5826 (Hebrew = azar) azar = prime root: to surround, ie, protect or aid: help, succour

Gesenius adds that the primary idea lies in girding, surrounding, hence defending

MEET

(Hebrew = kenegdo) corresponding to, counterpart to, equal to matching

"The traditional teaching for the woman as help (meet) is that of assistant or helper subservient to the one being helped. This definition would appear to line up with Strong's definition of the word. However, if you look at the context of every other use of the word 'ezer' in the scripture, you will see that ezer refers to either God or military allies. In all other cases, the one giving the help is superior to the one receiving the help.
Adding kenegdo (meet) modifies the meaning to that of equal rather than superior status. Scripture is so awesome. God says just what He means."

God's design for women is to aid our husbands in everyday life. Ensuring that the home is running smoothly so that he can have the confidence and freedom to do God's will in his own life.

A virtuous woman is a crown to her husband, but an odious woman shames her husband and rots his bones (Proverbs 12:4).

So what does this mean for us today? While our husbands may not be meeting elders at the city gate, he will be among co-workers, friends and church family. Are you ensuring that your home is a place of refuge for your husband? Or, is it filled with strife and stress? If it is the latter, how can you make changes so that your husband feels confident that the home is being managed and he is free to worry about his work and ministries?

One thing that I have found is that while we, as women, wives and mothers, often have crazy and stressful days and want to dump it all on our husbands when they walk in the door that is not holding our husbands up. I get it. We need to get it off our chests how rotten the kids were, that the dishwasher is broken or that so and so did this to so and so, but I implore you to give him some time to relax before pouring out all of your troubles to him when he walks through the door.

Set aside time daily to discuss any issues in a calm way when both of you have some alone time. Ask God to give you a quiet and gentle spirit when talking with your husbands. If not, you are simply sharing the stress and transferring it to him. How can he be respected "at the city gate" when he is stressed over all of the problems in the household?

Most husbands will, of course, want to come to their wife's rescue and will willingly take on their troubles. Try to give your husband some space and when possible, try to solve issues before getting him involved. Of course, never keep anything from him, but do your best not to transfer your stress to him.

Her husband is respected at the city gate, where he takes his seat among the elders of the land. Proverbs 31:23

Study Guide

How does this verse apply to today's world?

How does it apply to your husband?

What can you do to ensure that your husband is "respected at the city gate"?

Is God shining a light on any area of your life and how you respect your husband? Describe below what He is telling and what changes you need to make.

What else is God telling you about applying this verse to your life?

She makes linen garments and sells them,

and supplies the merchants with sashes.

Proverbs 31:24

Is the Virtuous Wife a Homemaker or Business Woman?

Through our study of Proverbs 31, verse by verse, we are learning quite a bit about this virtuous wife. In verse 21, we found that "She makes coverings for her bed; she is clothed in fine linen and purple." Here, we learn that "She makes linen garments and sells them, and supplies the merchants with sashes." How are these verses different?

First, the use of the word linen in verse 24 is different from that used in verse 22. In verse 24, fine linen is 'sindonem' or 'sadin'. It represents a finished garment of high quality. In the previous verse, the fine linen denotes bed coverings and other finished goods, as well as tapestries. The high quality garments fetch high prices and can be used for selling to increase the family coffers.

Not only is this virtuous wife an accomplished seamstress, but she is a shrewd business woman, too.

Let's look deeper at her business acumen:

This virtuous wife:

1. Creates goods that are needed (and wanted) by others

2. Creates high quality goods

3. Sells her goods and products to the public or to the merchants so that they are available to those who need them

4. Earns a reasonable profit to the benefit of their family (her family and their well-being are always her first priority).

This example shows us clearly that being a biblical ideal wife is not limited to stay-at-home wives and moms. but also those that work out of the home, as well. (Or work from home). God has a plan for each of us. We all have different gifts and callings in life. We are each called to serve in different ways - at home, at church, in ministry and in our professions. Some of us are called to serve at home. Some women are called to work outside the home, perhaps to be salt and light in the midst of sin.

What I take from this is that each of us are called to something different. God prepares us and then He uses us to carry out His will. So many Christian women that I encounter feel that they cannot be the ideal biblical wife if they are not full-time homemakers. This is hogwash! While the woman described in Proverbs 31 is a full-time homemaker, she still contributes to the family finances by selling her goods. While you may need to work outside the home (or simply want to), you can be just as effective as a Proverbs 31 wife as a full-time homemaker can. Your days will look a bit different and you may need to juggle a bit more, but you are just as valuable, just as called and have the opportunity to impact lives for Christ outside of the home.

The only caution that I see is not to take your eyes off the fact that our first ministry is in the home. Family needs should come first (after God, of course!), and then other priorities can follow.

The woman of noble character is ingenious and industrious. She is intelligent and diligent. She sees business opportunities and leverages them for the benefit of the family home and bank account. She puts her domestic duties first, serving her husband and children, but has a drive and a passion to contribute in other ways.

She is an enterprising woman. While she may enjoy being a homemaker and thrive at it, she strives to use her talents in other ways. In Proverbs 31:24, she creates and sells fine linens. In today's world, she may be in direct sales, online coaching, or work outside the home. This woman is entrepreneurial and may be ambitious in her passion to serve her husband and family.

Study Guide

Do you think you can be a virtuous wife and work outside the home? Why or why not?

How do you think the virtuous wife is called to serve if she works in a professional capacity?

How do you feel that you are called to serve?

What is God telling you about how to apply this verse to your life?

She is clothed with strength and dignity;

she can laugh at the days to come.

Proverbs 31:25

She is Clothed with Strength and Dignity

In several prior verses from this chapter, we learn that the Proverbs 31 woman makes clothing and garments for herself, her family and others (she makes coverings for her bed; she is clothed in fine linen and purple.in Proverbs 31:22, for example), but in this verse we see a glimpse of her "spiritual clothing". There are several references throughout the Bible on what we "put on" ourselves or "clothing yourself with Christ" (for all of you who were baptized into Christ have clothed yourselves with Christ. - Galatians 3:27).

When we first believed, we were clothed with Christ and became children of God through faith. We put on our clothing of strength and dignity by growing in our faith and asking the Holy Spirit to work in us (Galatians 5:16-26)

We also find a reference to clothing ourselves with strength in Isaiah 52:1 - *Awake, awake, Zion, clothe yourself with strength! Put on your garments of splendor, Jerusalem, the holy city. The uncircumcised and defiled will not enter you again.*

It is God's desire for us as Christian women for us to wrap ourselves in honor, inner beauty and strength. We can do this through seeking God in all we do and studying His Word to learn how He wants us to live. All around us in today's world are things that are not of God. We see and hear the worldview on television, music, in the workplace and goodness, even on Facebook. It is only by truly seeking Him and surrounding ourselves with things (and people) of God that we can clothe ourselves in strength and dignity.

Little steps such as listening to Christian music and spending time with other believers can help draw us closer to Him and further from worldviews. We can never escape the worldview altogether, unless we want to live in a remote cabin with no neighbors or technology, but we can take practical steps to intimately know and seek God.

The second part of this verse, "*she can laugh at the days to come*" also comes from knowing and seeking God. Because this virtuous woman seeks God in all her steps, she is not afraid for the future or anxious about anything.

As said in Matthew 6:34, she lets "*tomorrow worry about itself*".

When I had my cancer diagnosis this past summer, my first instinct (I'm human, after all) was near panic. What if they didn't catch it in time? What is the prognosis? What if I need a colostomy bag? When I took a step back and began reading scripture about fear and relying on God and then praying over that scripture, I began to let go of the fear. I thanked God for this diagnosis that drew me closer to Him and provided the catalyst for me to encourage others to get early screening for colon cancer.

While cancer is no laughing matter, I was no longer afraid for the future. I knew that God held me in the palm of His hand and would take care of me - even if that care may not look like I had hoped. He was in control and that knowledge brought me incredible peace.

Study Guide

Are you clothed in strength and dignity? How?

If you answered no, why not? What do you need to do to change that?

Can you laugh at the days to come knowing that God is in control?

THE COMPLETE PROVERBS 31 WOMAN

If not, how can you place your trust in Him?

What is God telling you about applying this verse to your life?

She speaks with wisdom,

and faithful instruction is on her tongue.

Proverbs 31:26

Speak with Wisdom and Faithful Instruction

Ouch! I am going to be honest here with you friends. God is convicting me with this verse. When I pray, I ask Him to shine a light on any areas of sin in my life or any area that He wants me to work on. Well, my friends, he didn't just shine a light. He has a million watt spotlight pointing right at this one.

Now, don't get me wrong. I am careful not to curse and try to speak kindly to my husband and children, but there is so much more to speaking with wisdom and faithful instruction than not using curse words.

The words we speak have the power to build up or tear down those around us. Even when we aren't talking directly to someone, God hears us. Take for example, recently, after church, as we were walking to the car, I said something to my husband about a fellow congregant. Something along the lines of "Can you believe what a jerk he is?" As it was coming out of my mouth, I realized that, although I didn't say it to the man's face, I was not speaking with "wisdom and faithful" instruction. I felt God convict me nearly instantly.

My words were spoken to my husband (about someone else), but the words I speak can have a lasting impact on those around me. My husband heard me tear down, not build up another. Does he wonder if I talk badly about him to others when he is not around? **Are my words showing that I have Christ in my heart?** In this case, clearly they did not. Ouch.

Let no corrupting talk come out of your mouths, but only such as is good for building up, as fits the occasion, that it may give grace to those who hear. Ephesians 4:29

Harsh words, critical tone of voice, impatience, sarcasm, gossip, complaining, grumbling, yelling… there are so many ways we can hurt others with our words.

Be mindful of the words we are speaking

In this verse, the translation of wisdom in Hebrew is torah and means "direction, instruction, and law." Not a bunch of rules, but the law of mercy, kindness and grace.

She is teaching her family about God's loyalty, faithfulness, and the most beautiful of all: loving-kindness. The word used is the Hebrew word, hesed. (or chesed). She is teaching her family and demonstrating God's loving kindness with her words. Do I always do that? Ouch, again.

This Proverbs 31 woman probably talked about what was for dinner or what needed to be done in the home, but her most important words were those speaking in God's love and demonstrating His loving kindness. (hesed).

Before you open your mouth, think of what is about to come out and that God is listening, too. Does it build others up? Does it demonstrate God's loving kindness? If not, think about how you can rephrase your words or perhaps, not say them at all.

Study Guide

What can you do to ensure that you are speaking with wisdom and faithful instruction?

Do your words build up or tear down? Where do you need to make changes?

Can you think of a recent conversation where your words tore down? What would you do differently?

What is God telling you about how to apply this verse to your life?

She watches over the affairs of her household

and does not eat the bread of idleness.

Proverbs 31:27

Don't Eat the Bread of Idleness and How to Rock Your To-Do List

Over the course of this book, we have examined each of the verses in Proverbs 31, in-depth (10-26). (Verses 28-31 are to follow), but today's verse sums up the Proverbs 31 wife in one fell swoop!

The Bread of Idleness

We have seen her attentiveness to every aspect of a woman of noble character's life by caring for her husband, children, servants and even the poor. We have seen her wake early, stay up late and work by lamp, when necessary. We have watched her plant a vineyard, sew her own clothes, her family's clothing, tapestries and bedding. We have read about her selling goods to help with family expenses. As we learn more about this awe-worthy wife, we see that she strives for excellence in every one of her responsibilities!

The Proverbs 31 woman knew that her role as homemaker and wife was God ordained. She took this role seriously and she "slayed" it!

She did not idly sit by and watch soap operas (well, if they had TV back in biblical times) or let mountains of laundry grow. She was busy embracing her role as a wife of noble character. She did not "eat the bread of idleness", but was busy managing her home, her family and her responsibilities. She rocked in time management!

Let's unpack this verse, piece by piece:

"She watches"

In Hebrew, this is translated as tsaphah (tsaw-faw') "to look out or about, spy, keep watch".

This phrase means that she is keeping her family as first priority. She does not worry about the new washbasin that the neighbor purchased or what those crazy Smiths are doing around the block. She doesn't spend hours on Aramaic Facebook (hehehe what would THAT look like? :D). Instead, she closely watches her home, her family and prioritizes their needs and her responsibilities.

"to the ways"

The Hebrew translation is haliykah (hal-ee-kaw') "a walking; by implication, a procession or march, a caravan -- company, going, walk, way".

"of her household,"

In Hebrew bayith (bah'-yith) "a house (in the greatest variation of applications, especially family, etc."

Here, we see what she is watching over: her family's ways - their health, activities, and knowledge of God, what they eat, how they rest. She is overseeing how they live their lives, ensuring that it is good, and God honoring. She makes sure that they are eating their vegetables and brushing their teeth. She ensures that they have clean tunics and feel loved. As the wife who is worth more than rubies, she manages the home by taking care of her husband and family and watching over their lives.

"and does not eat the bread of idleness"

'akal (aw-kal') "to eat"

lechem (lekh'-em) "food (for man or beast), especially bread, or grain (for making it)"

`atsluwth (ats-looth') "indolence -- idleness."

Whew! Ok, this Hebrew tongue twister is so powerful! The woman of noble character is not lazy or idle. She knows how to manage her time and seizes the opportunity to work and serve her family.

She is the one who makes sure that the home (and family) runs smoothly. It is because of her watchful eye and her care that her home is clean, organized, well-fed and honors God. She (YOU, dear friend) are irreplaceable!

If you struggle in this area, don't fret. There are several small steps you can take to improve your time management. You can resist the urge to "eat the bread of idleness" and rock the role as wife and mom.

Here are my top tips:

Get Up a Bit Earlier

If you struggle with getting everything done in your already busy day, consider getting up a bit earlier. Just 30-60 minutes will give you the extra time to plan and organize your day and knock out some of your routines.

Reduce Screen Time

A July 2016 CNN report found that American adults spend an average of TEN HOURS per day in front of screens. While for many that includes work in front of a computer, much of it is staring at a smartphone or television. By reducing your screen time, you are gaining hours in your day. While I am all for relaxing and watching a good TV show, don't let screen time eat up all of your productive daytime hours. If this area is a struggle for you. Consider taking one night per week off from screen time and instead use that time to catch up on home projects or cleaning or spend time with your family.

Establish Routines

Many of us suffer from "analysis paralysis". We have so much to do that we don't know where to start so we zip from this activity to that without a real plan. This, in itself, can cause us to eat the bread of idleness! I encourage you, if you do not already have routines in place, to start an evening routine and work from there adding more, as necessary. I have written extensively on this topic on my blog where you will also find printables to help you establish the best routines for you and your family.

Second to meal planning, routines are the number one reason my house is in good order and maintains cleanliness.

Try Block Scheduling

With growing to-do lists that include everything from food shopping to cooking and from cleaning and organizing to home bill paying, there's no wonder we bounce from task to task, yet accomplish so little, at times. If this sounds like you, consider using a block schedule. For example, use Tuesday afternoon (or after work) to run errands, Wednesday you might block an hour out for household paperwork (paying bills, filing, reading mail, etc.). By setting aside time to focus on one task or a group of related tasks, you are more likely to complete the items on your to-do list.

Use a Planner or Calendar

This one seems obvious, right? However, the truth is that few people use them for more than a place to enter meetings and appointments. Find a planner that you like and use it to block out time for related tasks as described above. For some of us, having it in writing is the catalyst we need to ensure that tasks are done. I love crossing items off my to-do list. I may have even written down tasks that I have completed after I have completed them just for the joy of crossing them off my list.

I use a combination of Trello (a phone app and online platform) for my lists and a paper planner.

A few small changes can make a big difference.

Study Guide

Do you eat the bread of idleness? Is this an area that you need to work on?

If you feel you need to work on this area, which of the tips can you try today to help you to become more productive?

What routines can you establish to help your productivity in the home?

What activities can you eliminate to reduce the busyness in your life?

What is God telling you about how to apply this verse to your life?

Her children arise and call her blessed;

her husband also, and he praises her:

Proverbs 31:28

Motherhood is Kingdom Work

Wow! There were some days, when my children were growing up, that I could not imagine them calling me blessed. Some days they were rotten little stinkers and had me near pulling my hair out. Motherhood, especially Christian motherhood, is not without challenges, as I am sure you know and have experienced.

Most days, we are so wrapped up in the daily minutia of living - the laundry, the cooking, the shopping, the discipline that we don't stop to think about how it is all Kingdom work. Yes, laundry and discipline are Kingdom work.

In this verse, the Hebrew word for arise or "rise up" (קָ,מוּ ka·mu) is translated " as "to accomplish, to endure, to build or establish, to strengthen, to succeed." What a beautiful word picture! We are building, establishing and strengthening children for the Lord!

We are tasked with raising sons and daughters of the King. We are charged with influencing their hearts and lives. I am not going to lie. Many days it will seem like thankless work and, honestly, the goal is NOT to have your children rise up and call you blessed. Nope, it's to raise Disciples of Christ. If we do that effectively, one day they will dance with Jesus and THEN they will call you blessed for having led them to Christ.

In the meantime, we have this earthly mothering business to take care of.

Little ones may not be able to articulate their thanks but may show it in other ways: snuggles, kisses and those smiles that melt our hearts. When my youngest was small and we were teaching him to say "thank you", it always came out as "thankee". The words may have been off, but the sentiment was not. He was learning to give thanks even if it was simply for his bottle or a cookie. He was beginning to cultivate a heart of gratitude.

As my children grew, they probably said "thank you" a whole lot less until...they became men. Now that my children are grown, I hear, almost daily, "thank you, mom". Now the thank you's aren't for milk or treats, they are for life skills, love and lessons taught.

Recently, my youngest, who has a toddler of his own, texted me. He wanted to thank me for loving him and disciplining him. He said that until he became a parent, he had no idea how tough the job really was. His daughter, I'm sure, is the product of my saying, in my head, many times, "I hope you have a child just like you". She is as precocious and active as he was at that age. Now, he gets it.

So back to Kingdom work. Every action and every chore that you do, every word that you utter in the journey of Christian motherhood, you are doing to raise disciples of God. By providing clean clothes, feeding hungry bellies, saying grace before meals, reading your Bible, demonstrating compassion to strangers, attending worship and Bible Study - all are part of the job of Christian motherhood. All are daily demonstrations of loving others as God loves us. All are tasks that help your child to one day arise and call you blessed.

In Colossians 3:23, we find:

Whatever you do, work at it with all your heart, as working for the Lord, not for human masters,

The laundry, the cooking, the cleaning, the nose wiping, the reprimanding, all of it, do it as working for the Lord, not for human masters - not even your husbands and little human masters, your children.

The next time you are frustrated by tripping over toys or stepping on Legos (those things hurt!) or spilled milk or even mounds of laundry, thank God for giving you your children, your husband, your salvation. You are raising children for the Kingdom of God and that is important work!

The last part of this verse, "her husband also and he praises her" should not be overlooked here. How proud of his wife when she works diligently without complaint to raise disciples, manage her home and live an exemplary life for Christ!

Study Guide

Do you see Christian motherhood as Kingdom work? Why or why not?

How are you raising disciples of Christ?

When motherhood becomes frustrating, what can you do to remind yourself that you are raising sons and daughters of The King?

What is God telling you about applying this verse to your life?

Many women do noble things,

but you surpass them all."

Proverbs 31:29

Many Women Do Noble Things But You Surpass Them All

As we have made our way through Proverbs 31 and the attributes of the ideal biblical wife, some may be overwhelmed by all this amazing woman accomplishes. And, it IS amazing, but I would venture to guess that this incredible woman of faith is not accomplishing every one of these responsibilities each day.

Life ebbs and flows and we have seasons where one responsibility takes greater precedence over another. In some seasons, this noble woman needs to focus far more on motherhood than on entrepreneurship. In other seasons, she will be able to serve on more ministries than in others.

I believe that this verse, and all of Proverbs 31, is referring to how a woman carries herself in her role as Daughter of God, wife and mother over the course of her life. Not a snapshot of one day or even one year, but a reflection of her life as a whole.

Only Two Opinions Matter

While the last part of this verse states "*you surpass them all*" indicates that a Proverbs 31 wife displays a level of excellence that is rare, I want to share something important with you.

The only two opinions that matter are God's, first and foremost, and her husband.

Women have a tendency to compare themselves to other women and to judge other women. We really need to stop doing this. There is enough guilt for women who are, for reasons both in and out of their control, not able to run their homes, their families, their faith lives, as they would like to.

Some women would love to stay home with their children, but need to work outside the home. Other women have a desire to homeschool, but either need to work or have responsibilities, which prevent them from being able to do this.

A Proverbs 31 Wife is Unique to Her Husband

What works for you and your family, may not work for the family next door. Please do not judge others for their faith, marriage and parenting choices. And, don't listen to judgement from anyone else. In the very first chapter of this book, looking at what a Proverbs 31 wife looks like in today's world, I addressed that the role of the virtuous woman is unique to her husband.

If you are confident that God is pleased with you or at least your striving to glorify Him while you carry out your role of daughter, wife and mother, you need to be thankful and let it be. If your husband is pleased with how you carry out your duties, even better. If Mary at Bible study group takes issue with one of your choices, that is on her. Not you. Put away the guilt, my friend. God knows your heart and your circumstance. THAT is what truly matters.

The woman of noble character is a high ideal for us to reach, but certainly one worth shooting for.

If you aspire to be a Proverbs 31 wife, and to provide for your family through your gifts, abilities, resources and talents, then your husband and children will be blessed.

When your time on this earth has come to an end, you may even hear "well done, good and faithful servant".

We were created to be our husband's helpmeet and to love, care for and support our husband's in their careers and ministry. You may have heard the phrase "behind every successful man is a woman". I am sure that this is even truer if that woman is a Proverbs 31 wife.

Study Guide

How do you do in being a helpmeet to your husband?

What can you improve on?

Would your husband say that you are a wife of noble character? What makes you think that? If you don't know, ask him.

Do you compare yourself to other women and wives?

If so, why do you think that comparing is detrimental to your marriage? Your walk with God?

What changes do you need to make in this area?

What is God telling you about applying this verse to your life?

Charm is deceptive, and beauty is fleeting;

but a woman who fears the Lord is to be praised.

Proverbs 31:30

A Woman Who Fears the Lord is to be Praised

Whew! There is a lot to unpack in this small, but mighty verse!

Beauty and charm are not bad, but...

Let's start with the obvious: The ideal characteristic in a Proverbs 31 wife is the fear of the Lord, which shows itself as godliness and wisdom.

Society, for centuries, has held that the most important attribute of a woman or wife is her charm and beauty. Proverbs 31:10-30 was written by a mother to illustrate what her son should look for in a wife.

The son, or any man reading this proverb, is meant to take away that a woman's charm and beauty may be attractive and, because of that, he may think she would be a good spouse, but these characteristics can be deceiving if there is no character, or fear of God to back them up. Charm and beauty can be a form of smoke and mirrors. Things are not always as they seem and beauty and charm will not ensure marital bliss.

I am not saying that being charming or beautiful is a bad thing, but it is just ONE (or actually two) things. After all, God created and loves beauty. In the Song of Solomon, we read how much a man delights in the beauty of his wife. However, beauty, without character or a relationship with our Heavenly Father is not a good recipe for a happy husband or marriage.

Ishet-Hayil, A Woman of Valor

One of the beautiful things about the wisdom of Proverbs is that it can be applied to anyone in any circumstance. In 31:10, this ideal woman is called ishet-hayil, or the woman of valor. A title has significance.

The Hebrew word ishet (or eshet) is the construct form of isha (woman) and hayil (or chayil) means bravery (Psalm

76:6), capability (Proverbs 12:4), triumph (Psalm 118:15), a rampart (Psalm 84:8) or wealth (Proverbs 13:22). Essentially, the eshet chayil represents the virtues of courage and strength.

I adore the Jewish tradition that the entire passage (Proverbs 31:10-31) is recited by a husband before Kiddush on Friday.

The Bible is rich with stories of this woman of valor, but one of my favorites is the story of Ruth and Naomi. These two God-fearing women, mother and daughter-in-law, have found themselves homeless and without food. Ruth, the daughter-in-law, who in scripture is also called ishet-hayil, a woman of valor, risks everything to provide for her mother-in-law.

Her actions, which were selfless and brave, led her to her being "praised in the city gates," just as we also find in Proverbs 31:23. In Jewish tradition, many see Ruth as the perfect illustration of a Proverbs 31 woman. In this example, as well as throughout the Bible, we see stories of both queens and homeless women living a life that demonstrates that being a woman of valor has nothing to do with a woman's circumstances, and everything to do with her character.

So, what does the woman of valor or woman of noble character look like today?

A Woman of Noble Character Today

I think we tend to overthink this and make it a lot harder than it has to be.

I think the answer is a lot simpler than we make it out to be. The ideal woman looks like Christ. She is a woman who exhibits goodness, self-control, love, faithfulness, joy, gentleness, peace, patience, and kindness... She seeks justice, loves mercy, gives grace and walks humbly with her God. And no matter her lot in life or current circumstance, she seeks God's will in her life. She is resourceful and serves others in and out of her home.

Whether a woman is managing a castle or scrambling to provide a meal for her family, if she fears the Lord and is a woman of valor, she will live life in a way that reflects Christ to those around her.

Remember, friend, there's nothing wrong with beauty or taking care of ourselves to look good for our husbands (unless it becomes an idol that we place before God and our obedience to Him), but the most important asset in a godly wife is not beauty but faith in the One True God.

A Woman Who Fears the Lord

I would like to wrap up by looking at the phrase "fears the Lord". Clearly, this is pretty important to Our Father as the phrase "fear of the Lord" occurs twenty-five times in the New American Standard Bible (NASB). It occurs twenty-three times in the Old Testament and two times in the New Testament. The phrase "fear of the Lord" appears more times in the book of Proverbs than in any other book in the Bible. In fact, the Bible uses the word fear at least 300 times in reference to God.

The word "fear" in the phrase "fear of the Lord" comes from the Hebrew word YIRAH (transliterated), and it means, "to be terrified" (Jonah 1:10), "to be awe" (1 Kings 3:28), and "to have respect" (Lev. 19:3). The "fear of the Lord" is the reverence one would pay to a king because he is the majesty.

Proverbs says that the "fear of the Lord" – honor and respect for the Lord – is wisdom and it is the beginning of knowledge.

I love the description, written on GotQuestions.org about fear of the Lord:

A biblical fear of God, for the believer, includes understanding how much God hates sin and fearing His judgment on sin—even in the life of a believer. Hebrews 12:5-11 describes God's discipline of the believer. While it is done in love (Hebrews 12:6), it is still a fearful thing. As children, the fear of discipline from our parents no doubt prevented some evil actions. The same should be true in our relationship with God. We should fear His discipline, and therefore seek to live our lives in such a way that pleases Him.

Believers are not to be scared of God. We have no reason to be scared of Him. We have His promise that nothing can separate us from His love (Romans 8:38-39). We have His promise that He will never leave us or forsake us (Hebrews 13:5). Fearing God means having such a reverence for Him that it has a great impact on the way we live our lives. The fear of God is respecting Him, obeying Him, submitting to His discipline, and worshipping Him in awe.

Study Guide

In your own words, what does it mean to "fear the Lord"?

Are you a woman who fears the Lord?

Would your husband say that you place more value on beauty and appearance or on your walk with God? (Be honest and examine each area of your life)

How can you shift your focus from the world to the promise of eternal life?

What is God telling you about applying this verse to your life?

Honor her for all that her hands have done,

and let her works bring her praise at the city gate.

Proverbs 31:31

Is The Fruit Of Your Hands Honoring You Or Harming You

Throughout this book, we have examined Proverbs 31:10-31, verse by verse, line by line. We have been awestruck by this godly woman. She sews garments, cares for her family, buys and harvests land, extends her hands to the needy, and above all, fears the Lord.

We may have been inspired by her, we may have been intimidated by her, but, as I had explained in the very first chapter about this virtuous woman, she is unique to her husband and his needs.

The last verse, Proverbs 31:31 is a summary of this woman of noble character. The various tasks and responsibilities of a Christian woman as well as her virtues and characteristics. Let's take a closer look at the meaning of this final verse in Proverbs 31.

Honor the Fruit of Her Hands

"Honor her for all that her hands have done" (in the KJV it is translated as "Give her the fruit of her hands")

John Gill's Exposition of the Whole Bible explains the verse this way:

According to Aben Ezra, these are the words of her husband to her children, exhorting them to give her the praise and glory that is due unto her. Jarchi interprets it of the world to come; at which time, it is certain, the graces of the church, and of all believers, which are the fruits of the Spirit in them, and of their hands, as exercised by them, such as faith, hope, love, humility, patience, and others, will be found to honour and praise; and every such person shall have praise of God, 1 Peter 1:7; and also of men and angels; to whom these words may be an exhortation to give it to them;

What is the fruit of her hands? It is everything that this amazing wife of noble character does in the course of her day and week. All of the virtues listed in Proverbs 31:10-30.

You may read them and think, "Sheesh! All she did was work and serve others! She had no free time whatsoever!"

To that I say, yes, she worked hard to provide for and serve her family and others, but, Jesus said

"Whoever tries to keep their life will lose it, and whoever loses their life will preserve it."

Luke 17:33

The Proverbs 31 woman understands the paradox of the ways of Christ. If you lay down your life, you'll get it back.

Anyone who loves their life will lose it, while anyone who hates their life in this world will keep it for eternal life.

John 12:25

Our society teaches women to be independent to fight for rights. This focus of society has caused a downward spiral for marriage and women. This selfish thinking, less biblical and more worldly has resulted in broken marriages, broken relationships and lack of satisfaction.

If we lead selfish lives, the fruit we reap will not be sweet. Our actions, motivations and behaviors are to be sacrificial.

While the wife of noble character works hard, she is satisfied and blessed. According to Proverbs 31, she dresses well, eats well and has a husband and children who rave about her. Her husband, family and community honor the fruit of her hands.

She works hard to serve others and has laid down her life, but is she blessed!

"and let her works bring her praise at the city gate."

The second half of the verse "and let her works bring her praise at the city gate.", show that she receives praise in her community for the life that she leads.

Her proud husband will "let her own works praise her in the gates."

While "*her husband is respected at the city gate*" (Proverbs 31:23) , he does not take credit for her accomplishments. He will brag on her to his friends and associates for her contribution to the household and its success.

To wrap up our look at the Proverbs 31 woman, here are some additional facts about Proverbs 31:

It was written as a poem.

Packed with vivid and militaristic imagery, the poem is an acrostic. The first word of each verse begins with a letter from the Hebrew alphabet in succession. It is meant to praise the life and achievements of an upper-class Jewish wife. A woman who does much to keep her household functioning day and night by buying, trading, investing, planting, sewing, spindling, managing servants, serving others, caring for the needy, providing food for the family, and preparing for each season.

It was written by a mother to her son.

The intended audience is men. In fact, in the Hebrew tradition, it is the men who memorize this and recite it on the Sabbath as an honor to their wives.

She's not a real person, but an ideal.

Written by Lemuel's mom, this poem is describing an ideal partner for her son to marry. He should find someone who is adept at domestic tasks, takes care of herself, loves others, is resourceful and most of all fears the Lord. She is saying that if you look for a woman with these attributes, the marriage will bloom and honor God.

Love for husband and wife are not mentioned (nor is submission).

Love is a feeling but demonstrating love is action. When married couples fear the Lord and do their part, marriage can blossom and be fulfilling. Fearing the Lord means that love and submission are happening.

It's not a complete list.

Sure, there's a lot of responsibilities and attributes mentioned in Proverbs 31, but there are many other virtues of godly women mentioned in other parts of the Bible that are not listed here. For example, Abigail went around her foolish husband's back to save her family (1 Samuel 25) or Deborah giving military advice. God has gifted us each differently. Some are teachers, some are nurses, others office managers or musicians. We are to use our God-given gifts to serve our families and communities, not just follow a checklist.

Study Guide

What is the fruit of your hands?

Is the fruit of your hands honoring you or harming you?

What changes do you think you need to make?

What steps can you take to make those changes?

Do you think that you are "respected at the city gate"? Why or why not?

What is God telling you about applying this verse to your life?

Why the Proverbs 31 Woman Gets a Bad Rap

Whether you are a new believer or grew up in the church, you are certain to have heard about the "ideal woman", the Proverbs 31 woman. She is everything good, everything ideal. She is, among other attributes:

- Strong
- Hardworking
- Skilled
- Savvy

Other qualities of this woman include her "noble character" (v. 10), her trustworthiness and meeting of her husband's needs (v. 11), the respect her children have for her (v. 28), her "wisdom" (v. 26), her fear of the Lord (v. 30), and her overall industriousness and productiveness. These are all great qualities to have, yet, if we are taught that this is a yardstick with which to measure a Christian woman, most of us will fall short at one time or another or even daily! Falling short often results in guilt: "I'll never be good enough", "I can't be pleasing in God's eyes if I keep messing up" and similar thoughts.

You have all heard the phrase, "God doesn't call the qualified, He qualifies the called". I think this statement holds especially true for the Proverbs 31 woman. Let's look at some examples in the Bible of women who "fell short":

Sarah, Abraham's wife, was cynical of God's promise to give her a son and instead took matters into her own hands.

Deborah was a warrior woman and one of Israel's judges. She does not fit the typical stereotype of a woman who is a "*keeper at home*" (Titus 2:5).

Rahab was a prostitute, yet she welcomed God's people when they came to Jericho and her faith saved her and her family from death and destruction.

Priscilla was an early Christian and friend of the Apostle Paul, who ministered alongside her husband in preaching the Gospel.

See? Even our female biblical "heroes", were not perfect. And, dear friend, you don't need to be perfect, either!

I liken this to what happens in our modern world: We see the "Pinterest Perfect" woman with her perfect hair and make-up in her perfectly clean and organized home with polite and obedient children who never talk back to their mothers. We think, "Why can't my life be like that?" When we read about the Proverbs 31 woman, many of us have the same thoughts.

Crosswalk.com writes: "Proverbs 31 is a beautiful blueprint of a Godly woman, and one that we should seek to emulate. We should never forget, however, that our worth does not come from meeting any standard, but from the work that Christ has already done on our behalf and the love He is always ready to pour out on us, whether we feel we deserve it or not."

I have heard time and time again that the Proverbs 31 woman is not realistic in today's world. While we may not spin our own yarn or harvest our own wheat, we should always endeavor to live the Proverbs 31 life. We will mess up, we will fail, and we will feel discouraged. We are human.

It is okay to strive to be a better wife, a better mother, a better homemaker and woman. It is better than okay, it is great, but we will never be perfect. God created us with imperfections so that we learn to rely on Him for all we need.

I think that, in order to fully understand how God is using us for His good work and for His purpose, we must stop obsessing over what it means to be an ideal woman of God and instead focus on what it means to be the imperfect, makes mistakes kind of woman that God created us to be.

Instead of being discouraged about our failure to achieve the standards of the Proverbs 31 woman, we should instead remember the perfectly imperfect women in the Bible who have made mistakes but still take their place among those who have made mistakes, have been sometimes rebellious, yet stand as examples of women who have pleased God and helped to advance His kingdom..

God's ways are not our own. We will never understand His mighty ways or his unfailing love for us. Rather than kicking yourself when you are down or have made mistakes in your quest to be the biblical Proverbs 31 woman, thank God for your flaws and mistakes. Thank Him for those mistakes that remind you of your need for Him.

Yes, continue to strive to be a better daughter of the King, a better wife and a better homemaker, but keep your eyes on Him and He will lead you.

Study Guide

Do you believe that living a Proverbs 31 life is possible today?

Do you think that the wife of noble character gets a bad rap in today's society? Why or why not?

How can you apply Proverbs 31:10-31 to your life?

What impact do you think feminism has had on the view of homemaking?

What is God telling you about Proverbs 31 and how it applies to your life?

A Word on Submission

What it Means to be a Submissive Wife

A submissive wife. Are you kidding me? You want me to be my husband's slave? You want me to do everything he tells me to do and bow to him? I hear it all the time from women in online groups and forums. Whether it is assumed that the wife is to be a passive participant while her husband bosses her around or that she is to wait on him hand and foot while he does nothing and barks orders at her; it's a common misconception. Being a submissive wife does NOT mean that you are your husband's slave.

To better understand what it means to be a submissive wife, let's take a closer look at the definition of the word.

The word submissive is defined as: inclined or ready to submit or to put oneself under authority of another.

Let's take a look at what a submissive wife biblically means.

Bible.org says The Greek word Paul uses here in relation to submission is a military term meaning to put oneself in rank under another. God has ordained the principle of authority and submission in a number of different spheres: Citizens are to be subject to civil authorities (Rom. 13:1; Titus 3:1); slaves to their masters (Col. 3:22; Titus 2:9); church members to their leaders (1 Cor. 16:16; Titus 2:15; Heb. 13:17); children to their parents (Col. 3:20); and wives to their husbands (Eph. 5:22, 24; Col. 3:18; Titus 2:5; 1 Pet. 3:1). Every time the New Testament speaks to the role of wives, the command is the same: "Be subject to your husband."

Notice that describes submit as to be subject to. It does not say to be a slave to. To be submissive means to put yourself under the authority of your husband. In Ephesians 5:25, husbands are instructed to, *"Love your wives, just as Christ also loved the church and gave Himself up for her."* and in Ephesians 5:22, wife are told to, *"Be subject to your own husbands as to the Lord."*

When a husband loves his wife as he loves the church and when women focus on their role to love and be subject to their husbands, according to scripture, marriage is loving, kind and harmonious, not abusive or a slave to master relationship.

Submission is a voluntary action by the wife. It is a God-driven desire to please your husband and act under his authority just as Christians are to act under the authority of the church.

While the husbands are to be the head of the household, the wife is not commanded to keep her mouth shut and never give her opinion on matters. She *"speaks with wisdom and faithful instruction is on her tongue"* (Proverbs 31:26) The wife can, and should, share her thoughts on important family and household topics with her husband but she should do so in a way that is pleasing to God. How? Choose your words carefully. Don't argue or try to prove your point just to be right.

In a biblical marriage, the wife is the helpmeet of her husband. She should support him and give counsel. Ultimately, he is to make decisions based on sound biblical knowledge AND his wife's wisdom and faithful instruction. The wife is to support her husband and back his decisions even when she doesn't agree.

While the Bible instructs women to confront their husbands regarding their sin:

1 Peter 3:1 NIV

Wives, in the same way submit yourselves to your own husbands so that, if any of them do not believe the word, they may be won over without words by the behavior of their wives,

It does not say that women should be quiet and use only their actions. The key is HOW women use their words. True submission is demonstrated in both words and actions. Wives are to submit to their husbands as husbands are to submit to God. Submissive wives are not doormats!

Often, I hear women lamenting that being submissive doesn't work in today's world or that the Bible was written thousands of years ago and that those same principles don't make sense today. I say "nonsense"! While division of labor in the home has changed drastically throughout history and varies from home to home and marriage to marriage, the Bible, and God, are unchanging. Husbands are still to be the authority in the home and act as the spiritual leader.

Submissiveness is not timidity, it is not servility, it is not subservience, it is not docility, it is not degrading, it is not a sign of weakness.

Submission is a sign of strength, not of weakness and a greater degree of submission requires a greater degree of strength of personal character.

Being Obedient To Your Husband Means:

- Supporting his decisions even when you don't agree
- Following his spiritual lead
- Having a heart toward satisfying your husband

Being a submissive wife does not mean:

- Being physically or emotionally abused
- Being forced to do things that are illegal or immoral just because your husband told you to
- Going against God's wishes over that of your husband (For example, if a non-believing husband tells his wife that she cannot attend church)

How to be a Submissive Wife to Your Husband:

1. Serve Him First

Whether putting dinner on the table or putting his needs above the others in your family, serving him first, demonstrates to him and your children that your husband is the head of the household. It is showing your husband the respect that he deserves.

2. Make an Effort to Take Care of Yourself, Physically, Spiritually and Emotionally

Hey, I know that life is busy, but I also know that when you are not looking or feeling your best, you can't give your best to your husband.

Get plenty of rest, spend time in God's Word and make an effort to look your best. I'm not saying that you need to be in makeup, a dress and heels every day. I'm just saying that when you make an effort to look and feel good for your husband, he will notice and your marriage will reap the rewards. (See this post on *Beauty is Fleeting*).

What can you do to ensure that you are taking good care of yourself and making an effort for your husband?

3. Make His Home a Haven

When your husband comes home after work, does he come home to you and kids clamoring for his attention? Toys strewn about the living room? Noise and chaos? Or does he come home to a smiling, welcoming family that is relatively neat?

Yes, your day may have been stressful, too, but I promise you that if you make an effort for your husband to come home to a calm home, it will give him time to "decompress" and he will react accordingly.

Your husband has been pulled in all directions at work and when he comes home, his home should be a place of refuge and refreshment, not more stress.

Studies have shown, too, that a disorganized home can foster stress.

What does your husband come home to?

4. Listen, Pray, THEN Respond Lovingly

Many men find communication to be difficult. When your husband does talk to you (be it about the weather, his favorite sports team or an issue at work), listen to him. Don't interrupt. Don't give your advice. Just listen. Then ask God how you should reply.

Just having a sympathetic ear will foster comfort in your husband to communicate more often.

He may want your opinion or he may just want to vent. Allow him to do that, safely. Then lovingly respond.

5. Give Your Opinion, But Accept His Decision

All marriages face decisions from which restaurant to dine at or major decisions like whether or not to relocate.

Calmly share your opinion on the matter, including your rationale for it, but ultimately, these decisions are your husband's responsibility.

Allow him to understand your feelings, but when he makes a decision respect his decision— even if, especially if, you don't agree.

God has given him authority over your home and marriage for a reason. Respect him and respect God.

He may fail, but don't use the old "I told you so". Instead, support him and repeat the process (listen, share, pray and accept).

6. Let Him Protect You

Men are natural warriors and protectors. Your husband wants to do that for you, too. Are you allowing him to?

God created men to be hunters, providers, generators/producers, fighters/warriors and to achieve, succeed and win.

Are you letting him fight for you? Provide for you? Or are you, like me, a naturally strong woman, and struggle with this?

I'm a get-it-done kinda woman. I see a need, I want to fill it. I see a wrong, I want to right it.

My husband, on the other hand, avoids conflict and is much more laid back than I.

When someone hurts us, I have to pray and ask God to help me let my husband lead and protect us and NOT take action, myself.

How do you do in this area?

7. Put Him Above Your Children in the Family Chain of Command (and Importance!)

There is no love like that of a mother for her child. I adore my children as I'm sure you adore yours. That is a beautiful thing. Until that love becomes an idol or displaces the role of a husband to a wife.

I know. I know. This may seem harsh, but bear with me for a moment.

We are going to address two biblical realities here. First, God designed marriage to be a three-cord strand, not a four-, five- or six- (or more) cord strand. In biblical marriage, God comes first then our husbands and ourselves.

While we are to love and care for and nurture our children, we are not to place them before our husbands.

In 1 Peter 3:1-6, we read that if you are a wife, you must put your husband first.

This means serving your husband his dinner first. It means buying his favorite snacks at the grocery store.

It means respecting his needs and his wishes. It means choosing his wants over your children's wants.

This practice not only pleases God, as it is how He designed marriage, but it is modeling a good, God-honoring marriage for your children to see.

When we put our children first, they learn to be self-centered. They learn that, even though the Bible says that the husband should be the wife's first priority, mom doesn't put much stock in that.

I encourage you to pray and ask God to shine a light on any area of your marriage and motherhood that is not pleasing to Him. It may be uncomfortable, but it is only through discomfort that we can grow and live a life that honors God.

8. Let Him Be Your Champion and Warrior

This is related to allowing him to protect you, but it goes much further. I look to my husband as my warrior, my hero. He comes right after God on my list of priorities.

In movies, the champion is adored. People seek him out for advice, action and protection. I seek my husband out the same way. He is my champion and my best friend.

Is your husband your champion and warrior? Do you put him first? Or is he just another mouth to feed and pile of laundry to wash?

Respect him in his role of champion and warrior. Your marriage will be blessed for it.

Prayer

Dear Lord, please help me to understand what it means to submit to You, Lord, and to my husband. The world tells us that submission is a bad thing. In a day where Your ways are not accepted, please help me to remain strong and live as the wife You created me to be. Show me what it means to submit to my husband in marriage.

Help me to remain humble and gentle. Please help us to submit our hearts to you, Lord. Thank you for the gift of Your Grace that lives in me so I can live as

You've called me to live. Your Word says that I'm to submit to my husband as to You (Ephesians 5:22). I need your help with that, Father.

Shield me from others who say that it is weak to submit. Remind me that submission is strength and that I need Your help to live that way. Please give me grace to face adversity and help me to look to You when I am faced with the opinions of others in this matter.

Father God, help me to use words that build up and not tear down and to be a positive, godly influence in my husband's life. Remind me, though, that I am to submit and not battle him. Allow me to see the beauty in submission and following what You say about marriage.

Heavenly Father, help us to keep our eyes fixed on You and to always place You at the center of our marriage.

Amen.

Study Guide

Do you agree or disagree with the above about being a submissive wife? Why or why not?

Do you consider yourself to be a submissive wife?

What does being a submissive wife mean to you in the context of biblical instruction?

Is there an area of your marriage that you struggle with terms of being a submissive wife?

What can you do to change that?

What is God telling you about submission?

Conclusion

For most of you, this was probably the first time that you examined the Proverbs 31 woman verse by verse. Most churches don't teach this in-depth. Sure, they mention it from time to time, especially around Mother's Day, but few go as deep as we have here.

As society, over time, has become more "me" centered, as Christians, we are called to make our husbands and families our first ministries.

I pray that this book has at least given you food for thought on becoming a woman of noble character.

Attributes of the Proverbs 31 Woman PDF

1) .) A Proverbs 31 Woman is noble. [Proverbs 31:10]

2.) A Proverbs 31 Woman is trustworthy. [Proverbs 31:11]

3.) A Proverbs 31 Woman honors her husband. [Proverbs 31:12]

4.) A Proverbs 31 Woman is hardworking. [Proverbs 31:13]

5.) A Proverbs 31 Woman is selective– she picks & chooses her battles. [Proverbs 31: 14]

6.) A Proverbs 31 Woman makes wise choices. [Proverbs 31:14]

7.) A Proverbs 31 Woman always has a plan. [Proverbs 31:15]

8.) A Proverbs 31 Woman is thrifty & uses her money wisely. [Proverbs 31:16]

9.) A Proverbs 31 Woman works willingly. [Proverbs 31:17]

10.) A Proverbs 31 Woman supports her family. [Proverbs 31:18]

11.) A Proverbs 31 Woman works hard. [Proverbs 31:19]

12.) A Proverbs 31 Woman is generous. [Proverbs 31:20]

13.) A Proverbs 31 Woman sees the bigger picture. [Proverbs 31:21]

14.) A Proverbs 31 Woman is crafty & creative. [Proverbs 31:22]

15.) A Proverbs 31 Woman honors her family. [Proverbs 31:23]

16.) A Proverbs 31 Woman is talented. [Proverbs 31:24]

17.) A Proverbs 31 Woman is prepared for the future. [Proverbs 31:25]

18.) A Proverbs 31 Woman is wise. [Proverbs 31:26]

19.) A Proverbs 31 Woman speaks kindly. [Proverbs 31:26]

20.) A Proverbs 31 Woman is watchful & busy. [Proverbs 31:27]

21.) A Proverbs 31 Woman always fears The Lord. [Proverbs 31:30]

22.) A Proverbs 31 Woman will receive praise. [Proverbs 31:31]

23.) A Proverbs 31 Woman will receive reward for her good deeds. [Proverbs 31:31]

24.) A Proverbs 31 Woman takes up for the defenseless. [Proverbs 31:8]

25.) A Proverbs 31 Woman doesn't wish bad on anyone. [Proverbs 31:3]

26.) A Proverbs 31 Woman has high standards & dresses properly/modestly. [Proverbs 31:22]

27.) A Proverbs 31 Woman is hopeful for the future. [Proverbs 31:25]

28.) A Proverbs 31 Woman greatly blesses others. [Proverbs 31:28]

29.) A Proverbs 31 Woman is worth far more than jewels. [Proverbs 31:10]

30.) A Proverbs 31 Woman has the trust & confidence of everyone. [Proverbs 31:11]

31.) A Proverbs 31 Woman brings good, not harm. [Proverbs 31:12]

Susan J Nelson is an author, speaker and the creator of Women of Noble Character ministries. She is passionate about helping Christian women live a Proverbs 31 life in today's world. The Lord laid upon her heart to serve women to grow in Christ, improve their marriages and manage their homes stress-free. She provides tools and resources on her website for Christian women to grow in their faith, deepen their relationship with their husbands and manage their homes well.

She lives in rural North Central Missouri with her handsome and hilarious husband and a myriad of dogs, cats and chickens.

Susan runs on Jesus, coffee and not enough sleep.

Learn more at www.womanofnoblecharacter.com

Made in the USA
Monee, IL
06 January 2023

24680897R00075